The
Spirit
Cries

Patti Gustav Xaviers

This book is dedicated to God,

Who divinely inspires all thought.

The human being is a masterpiece, whether a member of mankind is alive or dead. There are some components that come standard with the vehicle. Other aspects that make a human alive are left to an individual's freedom of choice. Let's first talk about the standard equipment.

The Body:

The body is the cocoon from which an eternal butterfly can find its way. It is the means by which man moves about the planet. The study of anatomy can reveal the details about what is known about the body. Physical appearance is determined by genetics. Our genetics are coded in our DNA. As we research more deeply, more and more is becoming known about DNA.

Some people are born physically handicapped, or become handicapped at some point in life. This may affect the ease of their mobility, but does not necessarily affect the other aspects of being alive and human. With advancements in technology, those with physical handicaps are better and better assisted as they try to move about in normal lives.

With the passage of time, a human body grows and matures from being a helpless infant to a capable adult. Humans come in two genders, male and female. Through physical union life is reproduced, and generations continue to replenish the earth with human forms.

The Brain:

The brain is located in the head. It controls the physical functions of the body and body movement. Some people are born or acquire brain damage, which may affect the physical functioning, but may or may not affect other equipment that a human is born with.

The Mind:

The mind is located in the brain. It is the primary control center and link between the components of a human that makes him alive. The mind is born naturally curious and hungry for knowledge.

The Soul:

The soul is located in the heart. The nature of the soul is what determines the way an individual thinks and what he believes. Thinking is done in the mind. Beliefs are stored in the mind. People can be born with "good" hearts. To be good of heart is something that can also be acquired and learned as an individual ages.

The Spirit:

The spirit of a human being is located within the spine. It is the living part of a human that can live eternally. The spirit perceives. A human being is not consciously aware of his spirit, but his behavior is determined by reactions to what is perceived by the spirit. The spirit is born with one objective: to attain eternal life. It is not born with the know how. From the moment of birth, the spirit constantly queries the mind in an effort to perceive whether or not the individual has figured out how to achieve life eternal yet.

The spirit is alive and active for as long as a human being is not dead. Based on the perceptions made from its queries of the mind, the spirit becomes active and instigates the individual's behavior. The activity of the spirit can be measured on a spectrum. If the spirit could be seen, it would change color.

There are three directions in which the spirit's activity can travel. Straight up in a heavenly direction, toward serenity; to the left in a negative direction, toward anquish; and to the right in a positive direction, toward excitement. If the spirit perceives from its query that the mystery of eternal life is getting closer to being resolved and that it will eventually be able to achieve its goal, it gets excited. If the spirit perceives that the mystery to eternal life is getting deeper, it becomes anguished. If the spirit perceives inner peace and happiness, it becomes more serene.

Depending on where along the spectrum the activity settles, different degrees of behavior are instigated and a mental "state" can be defined.

The state that most people's spirits are in for the majority of time throughout their lives is a state of calm. The state of calm is at the center of the crossroads that the spirit can travel. There is a degree of deviation from the state of calm that is considered normal. Deviation from calm, normally, is called emotions. A calm state is neutral in color.

The perception of the spirit is affected by knowledge that is acquired, and in the mind at the time of query, from the circumstances of an individual's life that either happen or do not happen, depending on what the individual expects to happen or is surprised with. If activity is stimulated, an individual becomes emotional. The spirit changes from neutral to violet in color.

Emotions can be positive or negative within a range. In a negative direction, normal emotions go to the extreme of being in grief or anguish to the point of physical tears. This can be caused by the loss of a loved one or physical pain. In a positive direction, normal emotions go to the extreme of being excited or happy to the point of physical tears. This can be caused by the introduction of a new love object or improvement of physical appearance, for example.

When spiritual activity goes beyond the range of normal emotions, it is unusually or abnormally overactive. On the spectrum the colors would go from indigo to orange, depending upon the degree of over-activity. The individual is no longer "emotional." This is "mental illness", and resultant behaviors constitute a physical reaction to unusual or abnormal activity of the spirit.

In a negative direction, the color indigo would constitute a mild depression. As the spectrum moves toward the color orange, depression deepens and moves toward paranoia. Extreme paranoia would be the outskirts of the color orange, on the verge of turning red.

In a positive direction, the color indigo would constitute mild mania moving toward severe mania to delusions of grandeur. Extreme delusions of grandeur would be the color orange, on the verge of turning red.

Beyond mental illness, which is a physical reaction but the spirit is still able to communicate with the mind, there is sickness of the mind itself. Sickness of the mind is the color red, and the spirit can no longer communicate with the sick mind.

If the spirit is stimulated toward serenity, the direction it innately wants to go, it starts turning white. The spirit starts to turn white based on things an individual does to get it going in that direction, such as praying to God or meditating. Both activities can make an individual feel more serene. Serenity requires action on the individual's part. It is not something that happens to the individual due to circumstances.

Before proceeding any further with this book, beliefs must be confirmed. An individual must believe in certain aspects that relate to religion.

Belief #1:

To fully comprehend and appreciate the concepts presented in this book, an individual must believe in God. An individual must believe that God is the Supreme Authority and Power over heaven and earth.

Belief #2:

An individual must believe in heaven. Heaven is the home of the once-earthly spirits that have already achieved eternal life. Some of these spirits serve as assistants to God and as guardians over currently earth-bound spirits (human beings).

If you can accept the foregoing beliefs, continue reading.

The point being made is that it is spiritual activity and movement in one of the three possible directions (heavenly, positive or negative) that instigates an individual's behavior.

It is normal for an immature individual to behave emotionally, within the normal range of spiritual activity that is classified as emotions. When a human being is young, it is the parents or human guardians of the youth who try to influence the emotional behavior through the application of comfort and knowledge until the youth returns to a state of spiritual calm. As an individual matures, his behavior, when considered normal, is more informed and justified by circumstances.

Now let's discuss the behaviors of the mentally ill.

When spiritual activity is moving in a negative direction, an individual begins to behave with symptoms, from depression to extreme paranoia. The individual becomes more prone to act in a violent and hateful manner.

When spiritual activity is moving in a positive direction, an individual begins to behave with the symptoms of anything from mania to delusions of grandeur. Behavior begins to become more bizarre, but non-violent.

If a mentally ill individual does not seek professional help and take medication, which can return the individual to a spiritual state of calm by using artificial substances, God's assistants and "guardian angels" may start to take action.

When God's assistants or guardian spirits take action, the individual can start to hallucinate and/or hear voices. It is the guardian spirits that cause these hallucinations and voices in an effort to try to influence the individual's behavior. The decision of whether or not to behave any differently as a result of hallucinations or voices is ultimately up to the individual. Spirits cannot force an individual to take any kind of action, but they can imply or suggest actions they prefer to be taken. If the spirits see fit, they may try to force to person "over the edge", from the color orange to the color red. Remember, an individual's spiritual activity that reflects the color red is no longer mentally ill, the physical illness, his mind becomes sick.

The color red is commonly associated with the devil. An individual with a sick mind is no longer in communication with his personal spirit. Because the individual's spirit can no longer communicate with the mind, it actually cries – whether or not the individual is physically crying. God hears the tears of a red spirit. The God assistants and guardian angels no longer have any authority over an individual with a red spirit. By forcing someone over the edge, the assistants and guardians have summoned God. At this point, God himself takes action.

God does not play with the devil. He does not speak. God influences the thoughts of other human beings that can take action against the red spirit on His behalf until the devil is defeated.

The extreme behaviors of an individual with a red spirit can be at either end of the scale. In the positive direction, the individual behaves in an extraordinarily bizarre, even though non-violent, manner. The negative direction is marked by individuals who behave in a criminally deviant, violent manner.

So much for the equipment that comes standard with the birth of a human being and the way the eternal system operates. Now let's talk about the aspects of human living that are freedom of choice.

An individual is permitted freedom of choice with regard to conscious decisions regarding certain aspects of his life.

He always has the option to use and/or ask for assistance in any area of his life. He has the choice of satisfying his curiosity and acquiring knowledge for his mind. Knowledge may be available to be taken advantage of or the individual has the choice of figuring things out for himself. There are times when the only choice may be to figure things out for himself.

An individual human being is given freedom of choice about what to believe about anything. An individual has the choice about whether or not to believe in and accept God as the Supreme Authority and Power over heaven and earth. An individual has a choice about whether or not to believe that eternal life is possible. The human spirit may have the innate objective of achieving eternal life, but an individual does not have to believe it or accept the existence of his spirit. An individual can choose whether or not to believe in the spirits that came before him in time and have achieved eternal life, and that these spirits assist God and act as guardians/police over the newly growing/developing spirits that exist within the living human beings on the planet. A human being can choose whether or not to seek serenity in his life, marked by feelings of inner peace and happiness. An individual has the choice of whether or not to cooperate with the eternal system and live eternally or end his life with the physical death of the brain and body.

So how does this all make sense and how does everything fit in? Here are some examples:

Like abnormal ("mentally ill") spiritual activity can be stimulated for movement back to a calm state by pharmaceuticals, spiritual activity can be stimulated toward states of over-activity/abnormality by alcohol and narcotics, including caffeine and nicotine. When an individual takes the action of consuming alcohol or narcotics, it is an action on his part and can therefore stimulate spiritual movement toward false feelings of serenity. Over stimulation toward serenity by artificial means can cause physical death. *Note: This writer believes that proper use of natural marijuana is a God given means to experience first hand the feelings of spiritual serenity that are possible and inspire introspection toward inspiration and revelations. Read: There's No Such Thing as "Medical" Marijuana – The Proper Use of "Pot" – by Patti Markow (available on Amazon).*

An individual can die physically or be killed by the doings of a red (mind sick) spirit when he is at any physical age or point of spiritual activity himself. The individual may be a red spirit himself, mentally ill, emotional, calm or even an individual working toward the achievement of serenity. When an individual dies before his natural time, God himself decides whether or not his spirit is fit for eternal life and either accepts the spirit into his house (heaven) or damns him (lets the spirit die with the physical body).

Jesus Christ is an example of a man who was able to achieve serenity in his life (ultimate inner peace and happiness that stems from a belief in God). He was murdered before his time. According to records, God accepted his spirit into heaven. The belief in the resurrection and rising to heaven of Jesus Christ is a popular belief.

Adolph Hitler is an example of a spirit that was mind sick (red). God responded by influencing the thoughts of other human beings to fight in a war against Hitler on His behalf until that red spirit was defeated.

The human spirit has a gender of male or female, regardless of the physical gender of the body. There can exist male spirits in female bodies or female spirits in male bodies. Hence, gay rights. Naturally, males are attracted to females and visa versa. It is a spiritual attraction that excites love. This explains two physical women being attracted to each other, or two physical males being attracted to each other. In this day and age, a male spirit trapped in a female body can instigate behavior to undergo a sex change operation. In this manner, the spirit perceives more positive vibes when it queries the individuals mind about progress toward eternal life.

As above, so below. The eternal system is not unlike the systems of government that are established in developed nations. There are police/peace keepers (guardian spirits) and there is a Supreme Authority, God. Human beings are the members of the eternal system's society.

Violence in today's society can be explained by the degree of anguish those spirits are feeling. Violence is behavior made by spirits that are mentally ill or have fallen into the red zone, mind sick.

By applying the concepts I have tried to express in this book to almost any aspect of life and existence that one is seeking knowledge about, that knowledge may suddenly be realized. The concepts that were primarily put into words herein are that 1) it is spiritual activity that instigates the behaviors of the human animal; and 2) how the eternal system operates as it relates to God and eternal life.

I humbly make this effort to express what I believe is divine knowledge that was inspired into my thoughts after I, for many years, applied the best of my learned knowledge and prayed for something to make sense of and purpose to my own "mentally ill" life.

Spectrum of Spiritual Activity

www.ingramcontent.com/pod-product-compliance
Lightning Source LLC
Chambersburg PA
CBHW050921290526
45792CB00002B/839